P9-ELQ-406

CONTACTING
YOUR SPIRIT GUIDE

Also by Sylvia Browne

Books/Card Deck

Adventures of a Psychic
(with Antoinette May)

Astrology Through a Psychic's Eyes

Blessings from the Other Side

Conversations with the Other Side

Heart and Soul card deck

A Journal of Love and Healing
(with Nancy Dufresne)

Life on the Other Side
(with Lindsay Harrison)

Meditations

The Other Side and Back
(with Lindsay Harrison)

Past Lives, Future Healing
(with Lindsay Harrison)

Prayers

Sylvia Browne's Book of Dreams

Sylvia Browne's Book of Angels
and

My Life with Sylvia Browne
(by Sylvia's son, Chris Dufresne)

The *Journey of the Soul* Series
(available individually or in a boxed set)

God, Creation, and Tools for Life (Book 1)

Soul's Perfection (Book 2)

The Nature of Good and Evil (Book 3)

Audio Programs

Angels and Spirit Guides

Healing Your Body, Mind, and Soul

Life on the Other Side
(audio book)

Making Contact with the Other Side

Meditations
(also available as a CD program)

The Other Side of Life

Prayers
(also available as a CD program)

Sylvia Browne's Book of Angels
(also available as a CD program)

Sylvia Browne's Tools for Life

and . . . *The Sylvia Browne Newsletter*
(bimonthly)

(All of the above titles—except the newsletter—are
available at your local bookstore or by calling
Hay House at 760-431-7695 or 800-654-5126.)

CONTACTING
YOUR SPIRIT GUIDE

Sylvia Browne

Hay House, Inc.
Carlsbad, California • Sydney, Australia
Canada • Hong Kong • United Kingdom

Published and distributed in the United States by: Hay House, Inc., P.O. Box 5100, Carlsbad, CA 92018-5100 • *Phone:* (760) 431-7695 or (800) 654-5126 • *Fax:* (760) 431-6948 or (800) 650-5115 • www.hayhouse.com • **Published and distributed in Australia by:** Hay House Australia Pty Ltd, 18/36 Ralph St., Alexandria NSW 2015 • *Phone:* 612-9669-4299 • *Fax:* 612-9669-4144 • *e-mail:* info@hayhouse.com.au • **Published and Distributed in the United Kingdom by:** Hay House UK, Ltd. • Unit 202, Canalot Studios • 222 Kensal Rd., London W10 5BN • *Phone:* 020-8962-1230 • *Fax:* 020-8962-1239 • **Distributed in Canada by:** Raincoast • 9050 Shaughnessy St., Vancouver, B.C. V6P 6E5 • *Phone:* (604) 323-7100 • *Fax:* (604) 323-2600

Editorial supervision: Jill Kramer • *Design:* Ashley Brown

The author of this book does not dispense medical advice or prescribe the use of any technique as a form of treatment for physical or medical problems without the advice of a physician, either directly or indirectly. The intent of the author is only to offer information of a general nature to help you in your quest for emotional and spiritual well-being. In the event you use any of the information in this book for yourself, which is your constitutional right, the author and the publisher assume no responsibility for your actions.

Library of Congress Cataloging-in-Publication Data

Browne, Sylvia.
    Contacting your spirit guide / Sylvia Browne.
        p. cm.
    ISBN 1-40190-120-4
1. Guides (Spiritualism) I. Title.
    BF1275.G85 B76 2003
    133.9'1–dc21

                                                                    2002010278

                                ISBN 1-4019-0120-4

                        06   05   04   03   7 6 5 4
                            1st printing, January 2003
                            4th printing, March 2003

                    Printed in the United States of America

Contents

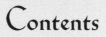

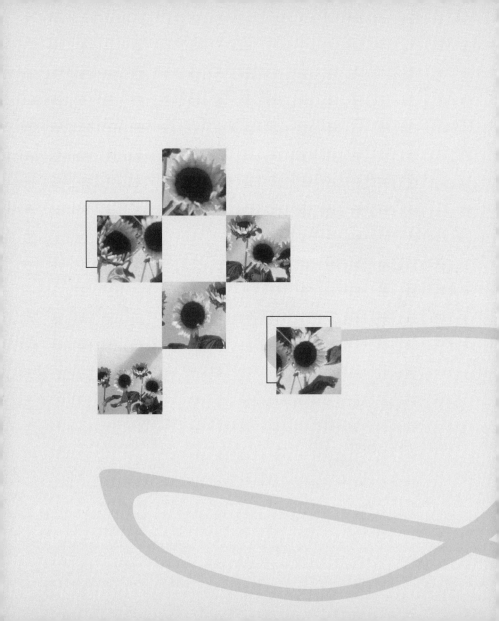

Introduction

I usually start out my books talking about how many years of research have gone into the publication of the particular work. While it's true that much research has been done in the preparation of *this* book, it's different from the others in a sense. The reason is that this book encompasses a personal story that's very close to my heart—one that details not just the reality of spirit guides, but the very real odyssey of my life with my primary guide, Francine, who's been with me since the very beginning of my journey in this lifetime. She and I made a pact, as we all do before we come into life, that she would be helping me along the way. In turn, she and

I would both learn for God and complete our mission in life.

We write our life's chart with the help of a group of friends, helpers, and the "Council," which is comprised of wise "master teachers," all of whom help us map out our purpose. Then, the spirit guide comes in to study with us and help as much as possible. After 66 years of being with my guide, Francine, I can truthfully say that she is my dearest, most treasured friend. Have I always agreed with her? Absolutely not! Have I tested her? Definitely. But I have to say that she's usually right, notwithstanding my sometimes stubborn need to argue with her.

I hope that this book gives you an insight into spirit guides—these often silent, omnipresent, patient helpers who have no other agenda but to get us through this life in the best way we can, and then go back Home to God. I had to laugh to myself when I read what well-known medium Arthur Ford's guide (Fletcher) replied when he was asked during a trance session if he would ever like to hold this position again. Fletcher responded without hesitation, "Never!" I'm sure that most guides often feel this way.

What people may not realize is that although spirit

guides are very advanced entities and exist on a very high vibrational level, they still have to be somewhat humanized. If they weren't, they really wouldn't give a damn what happens to us. So, of all the entities that reside on the Other Side, I would say that spirit guides display more human-type emotions than any of them. And I thank God that they do. After all, who'd want a spirit guide who acted like an unfeeling robot—with the attitude that whatever trauma you were experiencing would soon pass and that you'd forget all about it once you returned to the Other Side?

So, if you should ever feel abandoned and alone, I want you to remember that you are never without protection or companionship. Not only is God omnipresent, but so are Jesus, the angels, and last but not least, the often unsung heroes that stand patiently by—loving, helping, and healing us: *our spirit guides.*

Chapter One
What Is a Spirit Guide?

There's been some confusion for many years about what a spirit guide is. The differences in spirits do seem confusing, because we have angels (ten categories in all); we have our loved ones who have passed before us to the Other Side; we have ghosts who are souls who haven't made it to the Other Side and feel that they're still alive; and we also have what can often be confusing and hard to discern: energy implants. With an energy implant, there isn't any entity present, but a trauma is implanted by an individual at a particular place and time, and a psychic can then pick up the events imprinted in that soul's energy.

For now, however, I want to address spirit guides. These are entities who have lived life on this Earthly plane. They can be male or female and are very solid in their own dimension on the Other Side. You don't have to have a past life with a spirit guide, although some have. To put it in the most simple terms possible, you made a contract with this male or female entity to watch over you while you are in life.

Spirit guides study your chart (our program that we choose to come into life with) and help you decide the lessons you're here to learn, and also how they can help you do so. Many guides often study for a long time to be your guide so they can get your chart right. Of course you have help from the Council, too. The spirit guide will approach the Council before your birth and even after you come into life for advice and guidance with their charge (that's *you*).

Sometimes spirit guides have lived lives with you, but this is fairly rare; however, we must remember that everyone we know here is someone that we knew over on the Other Side. Guides can't be relatives who died when you were three years old or younger, because that would mean that you went unattended for a period of time. No, the guide is with you when you enter and is there throughout your life. The guide even helps to *take* you to the Other Side, along with your loved ones, angels, and souls you cared about before you came into life, but whom you have not necessarily known on Earth.

Spirit guides come in all shapes and sizes, and are from all different cultures. They can assume any visage, but I assure you, they're trusted, valued friends who will never disappoint you. They have great wisdom and courage, and you will hear from them if you're quiet and listen. Guides don't always have an audible voice, although the more you believe in their existence, the better they're able to communicate.

We get as many as 20 or 30 messages a day from our guides, but we have a tendency to chalk these communications up to our own thoughts, or to coincidence. That doesn't mean that you can't have your own infusion of psychic knowledge from God, but your guide certainly has a voice as well. What made you call Susan and find out if she was sick? What caused you to put on your seat belt the day you had an accident (something you should wear each time you're in a vehicle anyway)? These small and even larger episodes can very well stem from your guide. Unlike angels who protect and heal, your guides, as clairvoyant Ruth Montgomery once said, are "the nudging companions along the way."

Chapter Two
How I Found My Spirit Guide

Maybe I had an edge because I came from a long line of psychics (going back 300 years!)—but I actually heard my guide speak to me when I was seven years old. I was in my bedroom in Kansas City, Missouri, brushing my hair, and I heard a voice—high-pitched and somewhat chirpy, but distinctly female.

I will never forget the woman's first words to me. She said, "Sylvia, I come from God, and you have nothing to be afraid of." With that, I went screaming out of my room, down the stairs, and out into the backyard, where my grandmother (on my mother's side), Ada Coil, was working on a victory garden. In a flood of jumbled words, I tried to explain what I'd heard.

My psychic grandmother (a no-nonsense person whom I really looked up to) took a long look at me and said, "So? We've all had voices. Now, start pulling up the carrots." Later she did sit down with me, thank God, and told me that everyone has a guide. She explained that guides are from God, and our ability to hear them is somewhat genetic in our family. This helped a bit. I mean, knowing I was psychic was hard enough, but now I was hearing voices!

In the beginning, my guide didn't give me a running commentary, but she did give me messages. Please understand, this all started 59 years ago, and it was a much different world back then—one where people couldn't even begin to accept this concept—not to mention the fact that I was born into a Catholic/Jewish/Episcopalian/Lutheran household. None of this lent itself to making contact with a disembodied spirit. When people now tell me that they're struggling with similar confusion and fear, I understand completely.

I found out back then that my guide's name was Iena, and how my family and I got Francine out of this is beyond all of our memories. Maybe I just didn't like the name and changed it. Who knows? A guide's name is not really critical, but I've found that it's significant to at least know what *sex* your guide is and to have some identity basis. If nothing else, it makes them more real to you, and I'm also convinced that when we call upon them and believe in them, it helps the guide pierce the veil of the dimensions from the Other Side to this side.

Francine, whom I've received mountains of information from, has always stressed that guides are always trying to be recognized or accepted so that they can have easier access to us, thereby infusing knowledge into us or telepathically helping us fulfill our chart. People get aggravated because guides don't always make audible contact, but with patience, you *will* receive their messages, and if you follow the exercises that are presented later on in this book, I'm *convinced* that you will. Let me tell you right now that you won't necessarily hear the voice in the way you expect, however. It's not some soft, ethereal, melodic tone. Rather, it's high-pitched and has a fast, almost chipmunk-like sound to it. My dear friend, Lindsay, who has written with me for years, recently heard her spirit guide for the first time.

She called me one morning and said, "Sylvia, I heard Rachel, but her voice had a tinny, high-pitched quality."

I replied, "Well, that's just what I've been trying to explain to you all these years."

Francine says that's it's hard for guides to manifest and speak, much harder than it is for angels. Not that one phylum (particular sect of beings) is more advanced, per se, but since guides are on a higher, more elevated level, they find it difficult to tune in to the dense atmosphere in which we live. Francine describes it as trying to wade through a thick pea-soup fog. Over the years, I've heard the same story from people stating that they heard this high-pitched voice, and they've asked me to clarify what it is. The answer is simply: your spirit guide.

Strangely enough, while angels don't audibly verbalize, you can hear them in your mind, although they're not the talkers that the guides are. Also, your deceased loved ones can have a voice that you recognize after they pass over. Why? Because they were here so recently that they haven't ascended yet, after which it becomes more difficult to communicate. This is by no means intended to make you feel that you can't *hear* your guide; it just becomes harder.

(And since this is a question that is often asked, let me clarify: It *is* possible to have more than one guide, as I do—both Francine, my primary guide; and Raheim, my secondary guide, but usually you'll have just one.)

To go back to the name issue, I can't tell you how many times I've told people their spirit guides' names, and they've either exclaimed that this has always been their favorite name, or that they named their dog that name, or their mother was going to name them that same name. It seems that often the name of the guide can be imprinted in our consciousness. I've even had people come up with the right name after they "met" their guide during one of the meditative exercises that follows later in this book.

Chapter Three
There Are All Kinds of Guides

For a while there, it seemed that the fad or popular trend was for everyone who consulted a medium to get the name "Running Water," "Standing Bear," "Silver Fox," or something like that. Now I'm not trying to dispute the fact that there may be some Native American spirit guides, but it just seems that during my 49 years of research, I would have encountered someone who had one. However, as with everything else, if you do hear a name, roll it around in your mind see if it feels right, and then use that name—or change it, as I have. Just do whatever feels comfortable to you. Even though it makes it more personal for us to call a guide by name, I fully believe that it doesn't matter *what* you call them—as long as you *do* call on them.

Some guides will appear to us as children when we're kids ourselves. My son Christopher, whose guide's name is Charlie, came to him in the form of a child and grew up with him. Francine, on the other hand, always seemed to be about 30 years of age and stayed that way. This is somewhat aggravating to me, since I'm now 65 and she's still 30!

I've done enough research to believe that given my childhood (which featured a somewhat absentee mother figure), Francine took on the persona of someone who was older and matriarchal, while Christopher, who had a strong mother figure (me), might have chosen to have his guide be a friendly, helping child. Imaginary playmates are spirit guides 99 percent of the time. Guides will come in as children to make it easier for their young charges to learn from them.

Parents should be indulgent and even go so far as to set a place at the table for "Joey," "Sissy," or whomever the playmate may be. If we allow our children to talk freely, they'll not only tell us about their guides, but also about angels and past lives.

When my ministers and I teach Sunday school at our church, Novus Spiritus, we sometimes hear children go into long, detailed stories about their guides or angels when we tell them that God always has someone watching over them. Their faces light up, and the words tumble out.

This sometimes brings back a memory of when I was a child in first grade, and the nuns had flip charts that showed saints and angels. I remember raising my hand and saying, "I already know about them; I *hear* mine." I was promptly told to stay after school.

The nun who was my teacher told me to never voice that type of thing again. Even as a child, I can remember thinking so vividly that if you tell us they're there, and I tell you I know it, then why am I in trouble? My grandmother got wind of this and went to see the nun the very next day. I don't know what Grandma said to Sister Stephanie, but I was never disciplined again about this. But of course, the reason might be that after that incident, I kept quiet in class and only confided in a select few (who are still living today). I'd tell them plenty of things when we were alone together on the playground.

Chapter Four

Don't Rely on Your Guide to Make You Psychic

G uides can help you with your chart, your lessons, and your life in general, but their purpose is not to infuse you with psychic abilities. That gift comes from God, and it's your vehicle through which the record of your life and others' lives can be accessed. Can a guide like Francine tell someone's future? Yes . . . if she's standing right there reading your chart. But when *you're* attempting to be precognitive, it should be between you and God.

I still get asked to this day when I'm doing a reading if the information is coming from me or Francine. Well, it's me. The only time the information comes from Francine is when I'm in trance. I'm not trying to glorify or demean the trance state, but I'm not sure that it's something everyone would or should aspire to.

I had a hard time letting Francine come in and talk to me at first. This, I'm sure, stemmed from years of religious dogma being pounded into me—that is, the fear of being possessed and going to hell, and so forth. I still go into trance, and the information has proven to be very accurate over these many years. I've never known Francine to hurt anyone or come out with some crazy message. Now, you can certainly channel *without* going into trance. To tell you the truth, after an hour of Francine's high-pitched chirp, I'm ready to flee. But she can't help it—the sound quality, as I stated earlier, has to do with the warp in transmitting messages from their dimension to ours.

Let's Talk about Fashion

Some guides will appear in what I call their own definitive mode of dress. Some guides have actually dressed in Roman togas, but they can show up in regular street dress, too. Francine usually appears to me wearing a flowing chiffon dress. This doesn't seem to have any particular significance except that it reflects her own individual preference, which proves that when we cross over, we not only keep our own personality, but our taste in dress as well. My secondary guide, Raheim, is male and dresses in a white Nehru jacket with a white turban.

Francine began to physically manifest to me when I was 18 years old. When she told me in advance that she would try to do so, my family members quickly took up seats all around the living room. I began to see the folds in Francine's skirt; her long, tapered fingers; her tall, slender form; and a black braid. That was enough, and I closed my eyes. My family watched the full manifestation, but I couldn't. I've often wondered why I wasn't able to, and I've come to the conclusion that I was visionary and auditory enough, and besides, I had to live in this world. Yes, I have psychic ability, but I try to stay grounded as much as possible. If you don't, you find yourself in this esoteric, "airy-fairy" world where no one can enter except you. This leads to your doing things just for yourself and not for others. Psychic ability is bestowed upon you by God—and it's not supposed to be used for exclusively selfish reasons—it's given to you so that you can assist others.

Many years ago when I was living in a low-rent apartment with my kids, I was tucking them in one night when out of the corner of my eye I saw Francine in a fully condensed form. She was tall and willowy and had a black braid that hung almost to her waist. She was dressed in a flowing aquamarine dress that seemed to billow out. Her face was oval, with slightly slanted eyes, high cheekbones, and full lips. She smiled and was gone. It was as if she were saying to me, *You didn't want to view me earlier, but you'll see me now.* Sometimes when she talks in my right ear, I have an affectation of moving my hand in a waving fashion, which means, *That's enough now, no more chatter.* If I've given you the impression that Francine is constantly talking, though, that would be erroneous, because she isn't. She only communicates when she has something important to say.

Chapter Five

Do Spirit Guides Give Us Psychic Information?

Throughout all my years of research—not only with my own clients, but through the study of other mediums such as Edgar Cayce, Margaret Leonard, Douglas Johnson, Arthur Ford, and others—not one of them, including myself, can honestly say we've gotten much verbal psychic help *for ourselves.* The guides seem to be virtual fountains of knowledge for others, but not for the mediums themselves.

Spirit guides don't give us Lotto numbers or great insights into our future. Certainly guides will nudge us and give us some advice, and I'm sure they talk to the Council and help us behind the scenes with different situations, but as far as giving us personal, hardcore data—never! Now Francine will give me information about my church, Novus Spiritus, and spiritual knowledge, which helps, and she'll also answer specific personal questions in trance sessions for those who ask her . . . but not for me.

It's almost as if mediums are in a tube that allows information to come in for everyone else, but not us. If you consider this concept further, it makes sense, because if spirit guides verbally instructed us mediums every step of the way, we'd never make mistakes—and therefore, we'd never learn. If I do encounter anyone who gets specific day-to-day guidance, I'm suspicious, because life doesn't work that way. What would be the purpose of coming down to this Earth plane if everything always went perfectly? Mediums have to take their knocks just like everyone else.

Over the years, my friends and ministers have laughed

about this situation, and it has become a standing joke, because no matter what happens, Francine's statement to me is, "Everything will be all right." One day, years ago, out of sheer exasperation, I screamed, "Of course it will! I'll eventually die someday, too, and then everything will definitely be all right!"

I don't want to give the impression that Francine hasn't been right on the mark about some very important milestones in my life, it's just that, like so many of us, I didn't listen. For example, several months before my first marriage, she asked me, *Are you sure you want to do this?* You would think that this would have been enough of a clue for me, but no, I had to have it my way. Francine also told me years ago that I would have two boys and would end up living in California. So there are definite bullet points. However, again what I'm trying to convey is that the day-to-day verbal guidance that people may expect . . . doesn't occur. Daily occurrences are, nevertheless, imprinted in our life chart, and we feel them in our solar plexus. Remember, though, that the true infusion of knowledge comes from

God, so we can never, ever forget the Divine source.

Angels and spirit guides are truly the beloved messengers of God, and they are never to be replaced—not even by our loved ones who have passed over.

Chapter Six

Other Ways in Which Guides Can Communicate

Notwithstanding the fact that an ear infection or sinus drainage on our part may block a guide's ability to communicate, they do give us signals. They can create that hollow, dead-air feeling when external sound disappears for a few moments and the air gets still. They can also create a high-pitched whining sound in your ear. People have also reported that they feel a popping sensation in their ears.

A friend of mine was just dropping off to sleep when she heard a female voice inside her head clearly say, "My name is Heidi, and I wish you goodnight." She wasn't asleep; in fact, she was doing a very visual meditation about spirit guides. She sat bolt upright in bed and felt for a few minutes as if she were losing her mind. But that wasn't the case at all—spirit guides will simply use any avenue to make themselves known to us. Francine says that when the person a spirit guide is helping has a breakthrough, the guide experiences what we would call a sense of jubilation.

Now, as I mentioned previously, the guides are always happy, but since they have to become more humanized in order to be effective in helping us, I can understand why they get even happier when there's a breakthrough. I mean, think about it, what if you were always helping someone but there was never any recognition? It's not that the guides' egos are out of whack—it really helps *you* more than it helps them to acknowledge their existence. The guides are going to do their jobs, regardless. I also feel that it's good that the guides have lived Earthly lives, so at least they can have some conscious memory of the pitfalls and tragedies—as well as the joys—that life can bring us.

I've been privy to a light show that was presented to me by Raheim, my secondary guide. My then-husband and I took a trip to Kit Carson Lodge, near Lake Tahoe in Northern California. We were staying in an isolated cabin in near-complete quiet and darkness. We were talking about spirit guides and how they manifest. My husband then said out loud, "It's so dark in here. Why don't you give us some light?" With that, bubbles of light started to go up the wall and across the ceiling. Always being somewhat skeptical, I held my breath and didn't say anything for a few minutes. Neither did my husband. Finally after what seemed like an eternity, he said, "Are you seeing what I'm seeing?"

I affirmed, "Yes." It must have continued for about 15 minutes. The lights were in iridescent colors, flooding and running up the walls and ceiling. That's when you want to run out and scream, "Hey, all you people, come in and see this!" It had never happened before and hasn't happened since, but I have a feeling that it occurred more to prove something to my husband than to me. He had just come into my life at the time. While he believed as I did, he still had some real problems with many of the issues I dealt with. But from then on, he was a believer.

Perhaps the guides felt that if he was going to take this psychic journey with me, they had to give him a booster shot.

I'm very sympathetic when my clients tell me that they have a belief in God, angels, spirit guides, and an afterlife, but their families or spouses do not. Be patient with them. Everyone comes upon their own truth at their own time, and it doesn't help to shove it down anyone's throat, no matter how close they are to you. I always tell my clients to try to have their spirit guide give their loved one a validation. If a guide doesn't do that, then I advise them to believe quietly, in their own way, and not try to convert anyone.

It's amazing to me, though, that through my research, I've found in recent writings as well as in ancient writings, Biblical or otherwise, that in every religion, without exception, followers believed in prophecy, the concept of a third eye, and in the foretelling of the future; as well as messengers, angels, warning voices, and so on. It seems that the more technologically advanced and capitalistic we've become, the more we've lost our innate ability to get in contact with ourselves, as well as with the Other Side. Like "E.T.," we want to phone Home, but we seem to have lost the number.

Chapter Seven

What about Guides in Our Dreams?

My clients have reported to me more times than I can count that they keep dreaming about this same entity who appears in a meadow, a cloud, on a park bench, and so on, and will talk to them or give them a message. The clients ask if it is an angel, a soulmate, or a disguised loved one. It is actually none of these entities. Not that we can't dream and get a valid message from angels and loved ones, but the so-called stranger who keeps showing up and leading you through situations is your guide. I have a client who, when he feels distressed, will dream of sitting on a park bench, and a tall, very artistic-looking male will come and sit with him and give him advice.

The guide's help is not always as direct as you might think, which can be strange. For example, as I mentioned earlier, the message I got from Francine before my first marriage was, *Are you sure you're doing the right thing?* This message was more thought-provoking than a directive telling me what to do, and was also very profound, psychologically. I don't mean to say that guides can't get adamant, especially in times of extreme stress or danger, but most often they'll communicate with you in a way that makes you rethink what you thought you were sure of. I hear what Francine has to say, but I also ask God before I go to sleep, "Please talk to me, or infuse me with knowledge so I do the right thing and stay on my written chart."

A more clarified directive that came to one of my clients during the dream state occurred one night when she dreamed she was at a party. There were many people she knew there. Then, all of a sudden, a young man in a long robe approached her. She thought how out of place he seemed to be. Everyone was in evening wear, and here was this man in a plain muslin robe. He grabbed her arm, looked deep into her eyes, and said, "Don't let your son go to school tomorrow." She awakened and immediately checked on her seven-year-old. He was his usual, happy self. He wasn't running a temperature, and nothing seemed amiss, but the dream really nagged at her. Finally, she gave in and reluctantly kept her son home, the whole time feeling that she probably needed to check herself in somewhere for an examination.

At about 10 A.M., the phone rang—another mother called her hysterically to report that the school bus her child would have been on had had a terrible accident, that some children had died, and that the rest were injured. Thank God she listened to the message in her dream!

September 11, 2001

There are so many stories that came out of the tragedy of the September 11, 2001, World Trade Center catastrophe that it would take another book to report them all, but at least two people I spoke with had dreams that told them not to go to work that day, or to delay going to work. In a strange way, some were even *blocked* from going to work. Why were they spared when the rest were not? It's very simple. It wasn't their time, and their guides were making sure that they didn't leave before they were supposed to.

The blessed majority that did go on that day were the saintly sacrificial lambs who chose to make this world aware of our renewed patriotism, as well as our need to deal with the evil influences that were so profoundly affecting our world.

Chapter Eight
Questions for Sylvia

The following questions about spirit guides have been posed to me by readers of my books, by my clients, and by miscellaneous individuals over the years.

Q. How many spirit guides can a person have?

I've never found anyone in all of my years of research to have more than two guides. Even if that's the case, there's always a primary guide (like my guide, Francine), who helps

us with our written chart that we completed before we came
into this life.

Q. Can guides ever move objects?

Guides have been known to move things, but this is rare.
They are of a very high vibration, but they can operate elec-
trically, making lights flick off and on. I remember one client
who did an exercise to get in touch with her guide, and soon
afterward there was a loud popping noise that came out of
the speakers of her television—and then her TV was off.

Q. Do we ever become guides?

Yes, everyone gets the chance to be a guide. It isn't that
complicated, except for studying the chart with the entity. We
choose to help each other before we ever come into life.

Q. Why do some people have male guides and some people have female guides?

Well, Francine says that it's really related to our left and right brain. In other words, I have a female guide because I needed to expand my emotional side more. A male guide will be there if you need to balance your intellect. This doesn't mean that we're necessarily ineffectual in this area; it just gives us an extra boost.

Q. Can guides change our charts?

No, they can't really change our charts, but guides can help modify our chart, give solace during the pain, and often petition the Council to, let's say, give us some light at the end of the tunnel. Think of the guide as a trusted friend who unconditionally loves you and goes through everything with you, who encourages you, and who isn't beyond giving you a gentle but effective kick in the backside.

Q. Can guides heal?

Our guides can heal and help us mentally, but they always call on angels or even "spirit doctors" to assist us. Because they're so advanced, the guides have the ability to call on any and all entities at their disposal.

Q. Do guides ever leave us?

No, our spirit guides never, ever leave us. They're with us every waking moment. They do have the ability to bilocate, though. That means that they're able to be in two places at the same time, in full consciousness. This is hard for our finite minds to comprehend, but on the Other Side, our essence is so strong that we can fully be in two places at once. For instance, a guide could be watching over you and still be before the Council pleading your case to modify your life chart or get some advice or extra help.

Q. Can a guide be mistaken for a ghost or loved one who has passed over?

Rarely can a guide be mistaken for one of these entities, because they really don't manifest in the same way a ghost or a loved one who has recently passed does. The reason we see ghosts is because they haven't made the transition to the Other Side and are therefore closer to this dimension. In the case of deceased loved ones, it takes a period of time after they pass to reach the elevated vibration level of guides, because they've so recently come from this dimension. If the guide *does* manifest, it will be a brief appearance, like when I actually *saw* Francine and Raheim, but I've never seen them before or since. There's a real sense that they're with me, but not in full-body form.

Q. *Do people share guides?*

No, people don't share guides, although guides can visit each other or get information from other guides. Many people have even tuned in to Francine briefly at my lectures. When I'm speaking, I always have this strong sense that many spirit guides are getting together and saying things such as, *If you think* you've *got problems, look at what* I'm *dealing with.*

Chapter Nine

Shared Experiences
with Spirit Guides

I've heard numerous stories from my clients and others who write or e-mail me via my Website **(www.sylvia.org)** about their experiences with spirit guides. Following are just a few of the most memorable ones:

Karen writes:

I was lying on my bed one night, and I was in complete despair. My husband, whom I'd loved and trusted for 15 years, had found another woman and was filing for divorce. I was so despondent that I wanted to die. I couldn't even imagine life without him. Just at my darkest moment, my eyes traveled to a small pinpoint of light. I wondered how there could be any light in a totally dark room, but as I watched, the light grew bigger and bigger. In the middle of the light stood this beautiful man, tall with dark, wavy hair and chiseled features. He smiled at me and I heard him say, "Take heart. God has great things in store for you in six months."

I was still sad, but elated at the same time, and just as I was ready to respond, the vision disappeared. I told a few people, and they didn't believe me, but I know you will, Sylvia. (No kidding.) *In exactly six months, I met a wonderful man who truly loves me, and I've been happily married now for four years.*

Karen, this was definitely a guide who came to you during a time of great need. It's not often that someone will get a message foretelling future events, but due to your desperation, the guide probably got "clearance" to at least get a message of truth and hope to you.

$\backsim$ ❋ $\backsim$

Jason writes:

I was in my last year of college and couldn't figure out what I wanted to be. I had agonized about it for more than three years. I felt defeated and confused to the point that the depression was becoming overwhelming. My family seemed to be very irritated with me and was constantly asking me what I was going to be when I grew up.

I had been obsessing over a term paper and couldn't seem to finish it. I just felt all dried up. I laid down for a nap, and I was in that half-asleep, half-awake state, when a beautiful blonde woman appeared before me and pointed at my unfinished term paper. I couldn't understand what she meant. Later, when I came to full consciousness, I saw that at the end of the half-finished paper was the word "doctor." It was in my handwriting, but I can't ever remember writing it. I am now a successful neurologist, but often wonder without that visitation if it ever would have happened.

Well, Jason, it *would* have happened. Your subconscious probably took over and wrote it down, and the guide appeared to reaffirm that whether you realized it on a conscious level or not, your soul mind knew your chart, and your guide wanted to show up to validate what you charted yourself to do.

Brian writes:

When I was 45 years old, I had an unexpected heart attack. I was in intensive care and felt myself slipping away. As I did, I felt myself pop out of my body, and then I was above my body, looking down at myself being worked on by a team of doctors. I didn't seem to be that concerned; I was more curious. Then I became aware of a male presence in a white robe. He had long hair, was clean-shaven, but had the most compassionate eyes. For a split second, I thought this was Jesus, but then the figure approached me, and I got the distinctive impression that the entity's name was Daniel.

I asked, "Who are you?" He said, "I have always been here to protect you, but you must go back. It is not your time." With that, I was back in my body.

Brian, many people believe that they see Jesus, and it isn't that they don't or can't, because I have many letters that attest to this. Jesus, like our guides, is always available to us, just as God is, but because you got the name "Daniel" and the explanation, it's clear that you were contacted by a guide. The guide will often appear in times of stress, and always comes to take us Home to the Other Side during our final exit. It wasn't your time to leave this plane, and the guide made sure you didn't give up.

$$\backsim \!\!\! - \!\! * \!\! - \!\!\! \backsim$$

Janice writes:

> *One night, I was fast asleep when at about 3 A.M. I was awakened by a voice. The voice called my name and said, "Go to Joey." That's my nine-month-old son's name. I jumped out of bed and ran to his room, and there was Joey, pressed into the side of the crib. He wasn't breathing. I was frantic, but started to do mouth-to-mouth resuscitation. He began to cry. Now, the strangest part of this is, Sylvia, that yes, I was highly emotional and full of fear, but even after going through that unbelievable, almost fatal incident, I had the feeling that everything would be all right.*

Janice, two things were operating here. The guide called your name to help you save Joey, and the energy and peace that the presence infused into you helped you get through that trauma.

♋︎ — ❁ — ♌︎

Now, you may ask, what about the chart? Well, it was in her chart that Janice was supposed to go through this, and Joey, too. However, it was more for Janice's experience so she could be aware that she was being helped and protected. Janice might have needed this affirmation to prove to her that someone was truly watching out for her and her son.

Some messages are more subtle. For instance, as I stated before, we've all had an uneasy feeling about someone only to find out that we were right, or vice versa.

For example, there's a minister in my group who was going through a spiritual crisis, something that many of us experience, especially when we embark on the quest for truth. Although she wanted to be a minister, she felt that she wasn't good enough for the ministry, and she felt overwhelmed and unworthy. Rather than face me, she decided to e-mail her resignation. She tried three times, but it wouldn't go through. To test her e-mail service, she sent several other people e-mails about different subjects with no problem. However, when it came to resigning, she couldn't make a connection. *I* know why, and now *she* knows why, she was stopped from doing something drastic, and we thank her guide for this.

Christen writes:

My mother died, and I had lost my father six months prior to that, and then my fiancé broke up with me. My job was also in jeopardy. I went home after a long day at work and decided I was going to take a whole bottle of pills that I had kept after my mother's illness. I got myself all ready, got into bed, put a glass of water by my bedside, put the pills in my hand, and started to put them in my mouth. All of a sudden, there was a strong breeze, and it was as if someone flipped my hand, sending pills all over the room. I sat transfixed, and out of the silence came a sweet, soft voice that said, "Don't. God is watching." I decided then and there that there had to be another way to deal with my life. Shortly afterward, my life began to turn around.

These are pretty intense messages verbally, but without visual contact. So, the whole picture here is that spirit guides, whether nudging, blocking, speaking, or showing up telepathically, are going to use whatever methods of communication they can to get their message across.

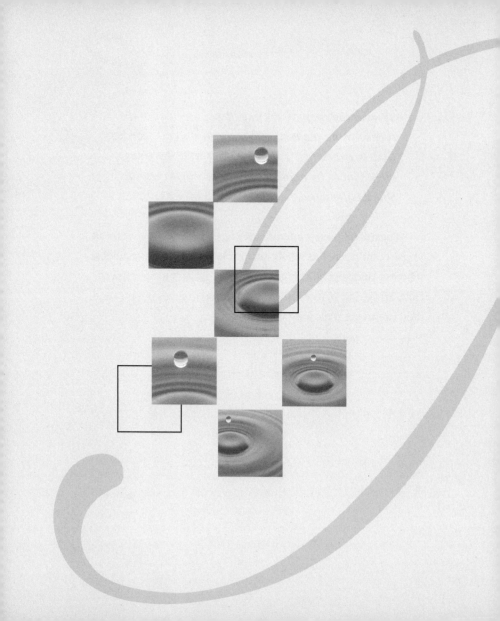

Chapter Ten

Exercises for Receiving Messages

The exercises that follow will help you open up your psyche to a greater extent, enabling you to better receive messages from your spirit guide(s).

Exercise 1

This short exercise really helps get the mind ready to receive messages, and it only takes a few minutes. Let's call this our training exercise.

In your mind, take yourself to a seashore, and put your back against a palm tree. Place your feet in the warm sand. Feel the sun on your face, the breeze in your hair. You can make this as simple or as intricate as you wish. Look up at the clouds and take three deep breaths, feeling all the negativity and hurt flowing out of you, down through your whole body, and out your toes into the gentle waves that are lapping against your feet. Then out of the shadows from the palm trees, ask your guide to come to you. Ask a simple question. Even ask their name. As time progresses, don't be afraid to ask the guide specific questions that you can later validate.

Exercise 2

This exercise flexes the so-called psychic muscle, getting your mind ready to receive messages.

Lie in a prone position. Visualize the white light of the Holy Spirit around you. Feel that a green light of healing surrounds the white light. Then put a purple light of high spirituality around all the lights. You are now totally relaxed, feeling that all illness and stress is leaving you. Your mind is quiet. Your body is quiet, yet rejuvenated. Your soul is expanding with each beat of your heart. You see yourself inside a beautiful room. The lights in the room keep changing colors from white to green to purple. All of a sudden, you're aware that there's a presence that has come up behind you. You're not afraid. In this expanded awareness, you have the sense that this is a presence you know and recognize. You don't have to see the visage right away, but you know this entity. This is your spirit guide, someone whom you love and have loved and have trusted your entire life. See if the guide will give you an audible message or even a telepathic message. Let yourself lie there relaxed. Then

count yourself up, all the way up to conscious-
ness, feeling absolutely wonderful.

Sometimes this is a good way to drift off to sleep. You may even awaken with a firm imprint of a message.

Exercise 3

I've used this meditation before in other books, but it bears repeating. This is what I call an active meditation.

Find a place in your home that's quiet. Get a
chair and place it in the middle of the space. Now,
put a white candle to the left of the chair, a white
candle to the right, a white candle in front of the
chair, and another in back of the chair. Light the
candles and then sit in the chair. You're surround-
ed by lights that not only protect, but that also
attract, the guides. Sit quietly and ask for your
guide to cross over this circle of light and give you

a sign. You may feel a light, feathery breeze or a soft touch on your cheek or hair. Again, ask a question and see if you get an answer. Stay in the circle for 15 to 20 minutes, relaxing, breathing deeply, and talking to your guide. Then get up, blow out the candles, and feel rejuvenated.

(*Please note:* Never let the candles burn all night, and always use containers that are flameproof to prevent fires.)

Exercise 4

This is another good exercise to help you open up as much as possible.

Take a deep breath and relax your whole body from your feet, ankles, thighs, pelvic area, all the way up through the whole trunk of your body; and up the neck, shoulders, upper and lower arms, hands, and fingertips. Come up the neck, face, around the mouth, the nose, and the eyes. Now see yourself in a beautiful green meadow. There are flowers around you. You feel so free and so alive. You're aware that you're wearing a robe that's loose-fitting and flowing. Your feet are bare. As you run or walk or float through this meadow, you're suddenly aware that right in front of you appears a golden door. You pull the door open effortlessly, and you see white steps leading upward. You start to climb the stairs. You get up about six steps and find yourself on a beautiful white marble platform. There's a purple mist around you. In the middle of this mist is the beautiful entity that is your guide. The guide comes toward you and embraces you. You feel so much love, peace, and healing. You descend the steps, and the guide comes with you. You open the door and run back across the meadow. You now come back to yourself with a feeling of protection and unconditional love, and you're more empowered inside than you have ever been.

You can use any or all of the meditative exercises above. The more you use them, the more you're becoming predisposed to not only hearing or even having a *sense* of a presence, but also receiving valid messages. The guides who know us better than we know ourselves are aware that we're "stretching" to get in touch with them. They, in turn, will stretch toward us, and together, this synergism will make it easier for the guide to contact us. Once the veil of belief is opened, the knowledge is immeasurable, and your life will be forever enriched by the loving guide who has been assigned to help you along the path of life.

Afterword

In conclusion, it would be a good idea for you to keep a journal. In the evening, write down all of the events, big or small, that seem to be beyond coincidence. You may be surprised by the questions you come up with, such as, "Why did I do that? Why did I say that? What made me have that reaction?"

Many times my clients tell me things they've said or done that were seemingly out of character. But were they really? Or was there an infused message from their spirit guide? Sometimes it's only later that we realize we were right about a situation or a person that at the time we had no conscious knowledge of.

I'm very avid about diary or journal writing because it accomplishes many things. Obviously it allows you to remember events, but it also enables you to recognize definite patterns. It helps to imprint your consciousness with the knowledge that something is definitely going on outside of yourself. It also tells the guides that you're trying to pierce the spiritual veil to make them accessible to us.

Spirit Guide Meditation:
Introduction and Transcript

Introduction

On the CD that accompanies this book, I answer some questions about spirit guides, such as: *Does everyone have a spirit guide? Where do spirit guides come from? How do we know if we are receiving messages from our guides—or just imagining things?* Drawing on my personal experience and the knowledge imparted by my spirit guide, Francine, I share the truth about these mystical beings with you.

I go on to illuminate the difference between angels and spirit guides, reveal techniques for better communication with them, and unveil the process that these guides must go through before they're able to help each and every one of us.

If you've ever wanted to understand more about the mysterious world of angels and spirits, I hope that this introduction will provide the answers you're looking for. As always, please remember that you are never really alone. You're surrounded by those who want to aid and protect you—and you have the power to ask for their help!

The meditation that follows on the CD can help each one of you find out who your spirit guide is and how to maintain contact with him or her.

Transcript of "Spirit Guide Meditation"

[Editor's Note: We have included the verbatim text of the "Spirit Guide Meditation" here (which is on the CD and is excerpted from one of Sylvia's lectures) in case you'd like to follow along or would like to refer back to it at a later date.]

Okay. So sit up straight, put your feet flat on the floor **[Pause]**, and it would be really nice if you just kind of put your hands in your lap with your palms upward. That's sort of like a way of receiving grace. And I want you to put a white light of the Holy Spirit around you. **[Pause]** And I want you to feel this descending of peace, harmony, quiet, and God-centeredness, Christ's consciousness that's always with us, Mother and Father God, and the love that Mother and Father God have for each other *creates* the Holy Spirit. And you can put anyone else in there you wish. You can put Bahá'u'lláh [founder of the Bahá'í religion], you can put Buddha; in fact, you can stack 'em. I'd call on *all* of them to attend you. And I want you to feel yourself very relaxed. And you'll get adept enough that you can even give yourself a code-color word—let's just use the word *blue*—which means that from this point on, that whenever you say it to yourself, you'll be right back into this lucid, meditative, *valid knowledge* of where you're going and what you're going to see.

And I want you to relax your toes, your instep, almost like you're *un*-stressing. Your ankles, your calves, your knees, your thighs, the whole pelvic girdle, up through the trunk, down through the shoulders, the upper arms, the lower arms, the hands, the fingertips. Up through the neck. Around the face, the mouth, the nose, the eyes, and the forehead.

And let's even go behind the eyes now. Almost like we can make it [the mind] escape, like so much dark smoke, not necessarily a blank, but a peaceful, quiet **[Pause]** vacuum. Not a vacuum in which knowledge doesn't come through, but also very much like the monks, who, by the way, shave the top of their head, their tonsures, because they felt that they could be infused better without hair on the top of their head. But let's say, my opening in the top of my head, from my pineal to my hypothalamus, to my pituitary, is open, so that I can infuse and bring knowledge in. Not random knowledge—we don't want to know that all the flotsam and jetsam in the world's gonna filter in, that we can do anything about—but put a codicil on it. In other words, only, dear God, what I can help with, adapt to, give warnings for. This also increases your psychic ability.

Now, I want you to *visualize* yourself in a meadow. And if you can't visualize it, sense it. And the meadow is very green. And all of a sudden, you're very aware that you are in light-fitting clothes. If you're a male, you are in a long robe like our Lord used to wear; if you're a female, then you can be in a gossamer robe, anything that's free-moving. You look down, and you see, in front of you, *white*. Brilliant white flagstone steps. They're not going upward, they're leading across this beautiful green meadow. With great anticipation, you begin to hop these stones. And they begin to wind around through this meadow. And you feel the sun in your face, warm, the wind in your hair, and you keep jumping the stones.

And all of a sudden, in the middle of this meadow, you see this beautiful, white, gleaming gazebo. It seems to be strangely not out of place, but it's just there. And there's something familiar about it, like almost that you were running ahead and you knew that you were gonna come upon something that was that beautiful. Shining, bright, brilliant. And you run up to this gazebo, and there's three steps leading up. But you don't really go up those steps; you stand there for a moment. And out of the shadows of the gazebo **[Pause]** steps a figure that appears at the top of the step. Take your first impression. Do not let *imagination*, the word, come in, the creation of your own mind. Let it be. This entity—tall, short, medium, whatever it might be—begins to descend the steps. And there is such a marvelous sense of, like we said yesterday, *Oh, there you are.* A familiarity, a feeling of positive energy, a feeling of love.

This person has descended the steps, puts their arm around you. You say to this person, "What is your name?"

Now, please don't be discouraged if it happens to be a loved one. Because a loved one can have, sometimes, priority, and *push* the person, or the guide out of the way, and show up as William or Ed or whoever it might be. Don't push anyone away, because whoever's the most prominent, or whoever you need, might show up. Your spouse who's passed . . . but many times it's a guide. Go with the first impression of the name. Even if it's not spoken—so much of this is telepathic.

Now with the guide's arms around you, embracing, you walk down the path again. The white flagstone steps. And right when you get about to the middle, before you get to the end, I want you to turn to the guide, and ask them any question that you don't know the answer to that you would have to validate. Please do not be concerned that they would be upset that you have to validate this. Even if you want to ask a question about,

"How long will it be before my finances ..." Don't expect a long verbiage right yet, especially if you haven't met them before. Say, "Give me a time in which my finances will be better," " ... that I'll find someone ... " and take the first impression. If it's two years, six months, three weeks, take your first impression.

And you continue down the flagstone steps until you come back to where you started.

Now, because you're going to come back to yourself, you leave your guide there, but that doesn't mean your guide is there, because you're just coming back to yourself. In your own dimension. But the guide stays right next to you. You've just gone on a higher plane to meet your guide, is all. But before you come back to yourself, you turn to the right, away from the flagstone steps, and all of a sudden, you walk a few feet and you see right in front of you, huge brass doors that seem to be just standing upright. Curiosity is a marvelous thing, and they have big rings on them, the doors, and they look heavy. But you take one of the rings and you pull it and, by God, if it doesn't just swing open. And you look down this long hallway.

You're barefooted, as I stated. And you find yourself entering this long hallway. And you're aware that pink marble on the floor under your feet is very cool. Still wearing the same loose clothing. And you run with anticipation. Even if you feel in this life you can't run. Boy, are you running now. Because the spirit can run.

And all of a sudden, you come to another set of doors, very much like the first, not as large, and you swing them open with no effort. All of a sudden, you're in a round room bathed in pink light. Pink light, of course, is always love. Pink is always love. Very pink. And all of a sudden, you, I mean your eyes, become accustomed to the pinkness of the room. Everything stands out in great relief. You look ahead of you and there looks like it's an altar stone. Like what priests stand behind, or now they stand in front of—and you find yourself circling this room and its heavy pink drapes.

Something pulls you to this altar stone. You run your hand, for some reason, under the altar stone, and your finger hits something that's metal, and you realize it's a key. Now you run your hand over the top of the marble, and there's a keyhole. You put the gold key in the keyhole and you turn it, and all of a sudden, the curtains part. And out of the curtains, almost like a stage, your guide steps. And I bet you anything, it's the same form, or sex, or personage, or sense of male or female—that might be all you get at the beginning, which is enough. And they guide you to another part of the room that also has curtains. And they open. And the guide directs you almost telepathically to ask any question you wish. Now here's what we're gonna do. This is when we're going higher up, just like that lovely lady asked me, "Is it from my guide, is it from God?" Because we have to have *things*, we can't just be nebulous. Eventually, you will be. But you've got to have the exercises. All of a sudden, a golden scroll drops. Beautiful golden, brilliant. Almost like you'd think of something that was written like "Ten Commandments." And your guide is sort of telepathically saying, "Ask God." You stand in front of this, almost like a sacred scroll, and you say, "Dear God, I want to know, dada-dada-da," whatever. **[Pause]** And all of a sudden, words begin to form: "How is my health?" "How are my finances going to be?" "What can I do to avoid anything that is health related?" "What should I do about my family?" You might get even the words *come, go forward more,* or *back off.* Even that, in itself, is an answer.

The guide has their arm around you, and now this is a room also in which you can find your loved ones, because they begin to congregate. Also, so do angels, because it's like a tabernacle. Because of the altar stone, you can make it as beautiful as you want. You can have it with a crucifix, you can have it with a statue, or you can have it just plain. But showing you two ways that you can infuse, eventually, you won't need a scroll, you won't need the guide to lead you, but we have to take these steps to get there. Now you turn around, and the guide leads you to the door. Down the marble hallway, the guide is walking with you. You're laughing, you're talking, and you can also ask them something. "How 'bout my depression?" "How 'bout my marriage?" "How 'bout my health?" "How 'bout my children?" And wait for an answer. It might be very short, succinct, to the point, that's fine. Later on, if you keep doing it, it'll get more elaborate.

Come all the way back through the doors. You've already come through the one set of doors, now you're going through the big doors. All of a sudden, you find yourself now—it's almost like a kaleidoscope—at a seashore. Oh my! It's so warm and beautiful, the sand is white. You dig your toes into the warm white sand, you feel the lap of the ocean on your toes. *God!* With such a sigh of relief, you lean back against a palm tree. It's like everything's melting away from you, all the pain, the worry, family, heartaches, hardships—leaking out. Going down your whole body, through your legs and into the water, and letting the tide pull it out.

From the right, again, out of the shadows, walks the guide. This is a shorter version. This is one you can use with the code-color word *blue*. Ask them, "What should I do about this legal case?" "What should I do about selling my house?" "What should I do about moving?" "Not moving?" "What should I do about my marriage?" or " . . . my relationship?" Don't get too complicated. Ask one thing at a time. And even if you don't understand what they're saying, the time will come when maybe it'll hit you right between the eyes, and say, "Oh, my God, that's what they meant. It didn't make any sense to me."

The guide comes over, sits with you, hold your hand, and more than anything, lets you know that whatever happens, they will never leave you. And at the moment of your passing, not only will your loved ones be there, but the guide will pull you through and out and take you directly to God.

Please do these exercises. They're very simplistic, and you will remember them. You can make them as elaborate as you want, as simplistic as you want. But you train your mind to get from one level to another. And the only way to do that is through meditative, active practice.

On the count of three, come up, come all the way up, feeling absolutely marvelous, better than you've ever felt before. One, two, three. . . .

About the Author

Millions of people have witnessed **Sylvia Browne's** incredible psychic powers on TV shows such as *Montel, Larry King Live, Entertainment Tonight,* and *Unsolved Mysteries;* and she has been profiled in *Cosmopolitan, People* magazine, and other national media. Sylvia is the author of numerous books and audios; is the president of the Sylvia Browne Corporation; and is the founder of her church, the Society of Novus Spiritus, located in Campbell, California. Please contact Sylvia at: **www.sylvia.org,** or call **(408) 379-7070** for further information about her work.

Other Hay House Titles of Related Interest

Books

*Crossing Over,
by John Edward

The Journey to the Sacred Garden,
by Hank Wesselman, Ph.D.
(book and CD)

Messages from Your Angels,
by Doreen Virtue, Ph.D.

Mirrors of Time,
by Brian Weiss, M.D. (book and CD)

Turning Inward
(a journal for self-reflection),
by Cheryl Richardson

*Crossing Over is published by Princess Books
and distributed by Hay House.

Audio Programs

Intuitive Healing,
by Judith Orloff, M.D.

Journeys into Past Lives,
by Denise Linn

Karma Releasing,
by Doreen Virtue, Ph.D.

***Understanding Your Angels
and Meeting Your Guides,***
by John Edward

Card Decks

***Healing with the Angels
Oracle Cards,***
by Doreen Virtue, Ph.D.

***Messages from Your Angels
Oracle Cards,***
by Doreen Virtue, Ph.D.

All of the products on the previous pages are
available at your local bookstore,
or may be ordered through Hay House, Inc.:
(800) 654-5126 or **(760) 431-7695**
(800) 650-5115 (fax) or **(760) 431-6948 (fax)**
www.hayhouse.com

Notes

Notes

Notes

Notes

Notes

Notes

We hope you enjoyed this Hay House book.
If you would like to receive a free catalog featuring
additional Hay House books and products,
or if you would like information about the
Hay Foundation, please contact:

Hay House, Inc.
P.O. Box 5100
Carlsbad, CA 92018-5100

(760) 431-7695 or **(800) 654-5126**
(760) 431-6948 (fax) or **(800) 650-5115 (fax)**
www.hayhouse.com

Published and distributed in Australia by: Hay House
Australia Pty Ltd, 18/36 Ralph St., Alexandria NSW 2015
Phone: 612-9669-4299 • *Fax:* 612-9669-4144
E-mail: info@hayhouse.com.au

Published and Distributed in the United Kingdom by:
Hay House UK, Ltd. • Unit 202, Canalot Studios
222 Kensal Rd., London W10 5BN
Phone: 020-8962-1230 • *Fax:* 020-8962-1239

Distributed in Canada by:
Raincoast • 9050 Shaughnessy St., Vancouver, B.C. V6P 6E5
Phone: (604) 323-7100 • *Fax:* (604) 323-2600